GW00500799

HISTORIC PLACES
OF BRITAIN

SUNBURST HERITAGE SERIES

HISTORIC PLACES OF BRITAIN

GARRY GIBBONS

SUNBURST BOOKS

For Ria and Merry

The publishers would like to dedicate this book and the others in the series
to Don Webb, to mark his contribution to book buying.

This edition first published 1994 by Sunburst Books, an imprint of the Promotional Reprint
Company Limited, Deacon House, 65 Old Church Street, London, SW3 5BS.

Designed by Anthony Cohen
Printed and bound in China

ISBN 1 85778 050 7

Cover photograph: Stonehenge, Wiltshire
Half title: Mên-an-Tol, Cornwall
Title page: Loch Ness, Highlands

CONTENTS

Introduction 6

ENGLAND

WALES

SCOTLAND

INTRODUCTION

The single most intriguing aspect of Britain's landscape is surely its diversity. To travel from the rolling lowlands of southern England to the majestic heights of northern Scotland is to experience a staggering geological transformation, the origins of which lie 2,500 million years in the past, at the very start of history.

At this time the land mass which was to become Britain existed as sea-beds of sedimentary rock many miles thick. Earthquakes and volcanic eruptions forced this subterranean mass skyward, twisting above the ancient seas to lay the foundations of the Scottish Highlands and Islands, the great peaks of Cumbria and Snowdonia and the granite base of Dartmoor and Cornwall.

The band of oolitic limestone running from Devon, Dorset and Somerset through the Cotswolds, Oxfordshire and the North Yorkshire moors formed 200 million years ago beneath the waters of tropical seas. The downlands of southern England are all that remain of the Great Chalk Sea which covered most of Europe 100 million years later. Countless layers of tiny, single-cell creatures collected on the sea-bed at the rate of one metre every 100,000 years. The carpet of white chalk is 500m thick in places.

Some 18,000 million years ago all of 'Britain' down to south Wales and the Wash lay under an ice sheet, which was up to a mile thick. This was the fourth ice age, the last in a series of glaciations which peaked every 100,000 years. Below the ice line lay a vast area of arctic tundra, extending down as far as Bordeaux in France. Beneath the ice, valleys were gouged out in the mountains of Snowdonia and the Highlands, whilst the hills of Scotland, Wales and north England were ground smooth if the rocks were soft, or carved into jagged peaks if they were hard.

It would be wrong, however, to consider the great volcanic upheavals and glacial grindings which shaped much of our present environment in terms of static layers of undulating debris. To do so would be a denial of the unique character of our collection of islands. Our landscape bears witness to the complex series of strands which are interwoven into the single thread of history running down through time to us today.

The natural progress of Britain's landscape may have continued unchecked, had humans not appeared some three million years ago. Little is known of those early peoples and the methods they used to forge a living from their surroundings, as most traces of them have been obscured by the effects of time and four great ice ages.

Human progress from 10,000 BC presents a clearer picture. Paleolithic - Early Stone Age - man arrived across the land bridge which linked 'Britain' with the continent. Armed with weapons fashioned from stone, he hunted the migrating herds of mammoths, woolly rhinoceros and reindeer which grazed the tundra from southern Britain down to Bordeaux in France. It was Early Stone Age man who laid the foundations of our system of tracks and roads which would later be extended.

The climate warmed, broadleaf forest spread over the land and the hairy ice age beasts gave way to the bear, boar and wolf. By 8,000 BC Mesolithic - Middle Stone Age - man was clearing sections of forest, building temporary dwellings and practising basic animal husbandry.

Up until this time the human population only numbered a few thousand, but, from 5,000 BC, this number grew to between 30,000 and 50,000 people, for Neolithic - New Stone Age - man arrived from the Mediterranean. These New Stone Age people were accomplished sailors and traders, and their boats arrived carrying wheat, barley and domesticated animals. They were also organised farmers, and undertook what was, at that time, extensive deforestation. Their knowledge of grain growing, animal domestication and agriculture set in motion a social revolution. Neolithic man also made his mark on the landscape with great ritual monuments, for this farmer not only venerated his dead, but also the cycles of the seasons.

The practice of burial and religious ritual flourished with the arrival of the Beaker People from their homelands on the Rhine around 2,000 BC. Indeed, their name is derived from the pottery discovered inside their burial mounds. The Beaker People also brought with them skills in working bronze. Their ability to work metal and make tools led to more sophisticated methods of cultivation which resulted in a population explosion. Over a few hundred years the number of people in Britain rose to about one million. Settlements flourished, as did fortified hill-top villages, each linked by trackway. Large systems of cultivated fields appeared, covering thousands of acres. This signified the start of the deliberate sculpting of the British landscape which would continue through to the Iron Age.

The iron-based culture of the Celts spread across Britain around 700 BC. Their activity in the smelting and working of iron was matched by their extensive felling of the wild woods in favour of farming land which their iron-tipped ploughs could rip through. Field systems which could be repeatedly harvested, ploughed and resown led to stable settlements. As the concept of permanence entered into society, a means of protection became essential to guard both property and land. As a result, more than 2,000 hill forts became a conspicuous feature of the landscape. But nothing would withstand the approaching legions of Rome.

By the end of the prehistoric period most of the landscape was being exploited by a large population. The great primeval forest had fallen victim to man's desire to cultivate the land, and the woodlands which did remain were carefully managed.

The four centuries of Roman rule brought a prolific growth in culture and communications. This intensification of all the progress which had taken place in the past 1,500 years was tempered by various technological, economic and political changes intended to curb the over-exploitation of the landscape which had occurred previously.

9,600 kilometres of roads linked the Roman towns which were an essential ingredient of Roman civilisation. The 600 or so villas which are known to have existed were of equal importance to the Roman culture. The Latin word *villa* simply means a farm. The introduction of more sophisticated farming implements and the peaceful era which succeeded the Roman invasion led to a further growth in the population to about four million.

Following the Roman withdrawal, British society fell into the pre-Roman pattern of warring tribes, which resulted in a decline in the population and a weakening of the economy. The chaos which was prevalent at that time paved the way for the Saxon take-over, even though the Saxon influx of the 5th century was modest in terms of numbers. Saxon settlements in the form of hamlets and farmsteads began to flourish between the 8th and 12th centuries. The strip field system appeared and would remain a recognisable form in the landscape right up until the 19th century.

By the time of the Norman Conquest much of England had been cultivated. Between 1100 and 1350 the population rose rapidly to around seven million, while most of the existing villages expanded and their field systems were re-organised on a much larger scale.

From this time onwards, much of our landscape remained unchanged until the age of industrialisation which is still unfolding. As wars and skirmishes shaped the man-made boundaries of our islands, so their remains lay scattered across the land and serve to remind us of the complex and varied relationships, which have evolved over the course of time to shape our collective character.

Garry Gibbons, January 1994

ENGLAND

ST MICHAEL'S MOUNT, CORNWALL
A Benedictine monastery was established here in 1044 by monks from Mont St Michel, situated off the coast of Brittany.
Once joined to the mainland, St Michael's Mount is now a rocky islet which is only accessible by means of a causeway at
low tide. The edifice dominates Mount's Bay.

Main photograph: TINTAGEL HEAD, CORNWALL
Birthplace of England's most important legendary hero, King Arthur. Windswept ruins perched high on the cliffs are all that remain of the 12th century castle built by Reginald, Earl of Cornwall, the illegitimate son of Henry I.

Inset photograph: DOZMARY POOL, BODMIN MOOR, CORNWALL
Cornwall's only natural lake, Dozmary Pool is said to be the resting place of King Arthur's sword, Excaliber.

Main photograph: BODMIN MOOR, CORNWALL

The great granite plateau of Bodmin Moor lies at the heart of Cornwall, and at the heart of the county's rich history. There are many reminders in this area of the Celtic Holy Men from Ireland, who introduced the Christian faith into Cornwall fifteen centuries ago, long before it reached most of the rest of Britain. The highest point in Cornwall, 'Bron ewhella' (Brown Willy), is on Bodmin Moor, as is the Jamaica Inn of Daphne du Maurier's famous novel.

Inset photographs: THE HURLERS,
BODMIN MOOR
It was long believed that these land-
marks had once been men who were
turned to stone for desecrating the
Lord's Day by playing the old Cornish
pastime, hurling the ball. Scientific
research has revealed that the site's
three stone circles date from the
Bronze Age.

MÊN-AN-TOL, CORNWALL
Standing between two upright pillars, a circular stone endowed with magical healing
properties for those who crawl through its centre.

DARTMOOR, DEVON

Once the centre of an ancient volcanic region rising out of a shallow sea, this wild country at the heart of Devon stands high on two plateaux. The entire region is rich in prehistoric communal dwellings occupied by Bronze Age herdsmen and their families. In addition to these Bronze Age earthworks, there are many standing stones, or menhirs, such as Spinster's Rock, Grey Wethers and the Scorhill Circle. No fewer than ninety circles of standing stones have been recorded on Dartmoor.

Main photograph: DUNKERY, EXMOOR, SOMERSET
Rolling moors extend to the slopes of Dunkery Beacon, Exmoor's highest point. It is referred to as a Beacon
because, like the Brecon Beacons in Wales, it was used as a site for signal fires in medieval times. The virtually
uninhabited region of Exmoor is the setting for Blackmore's famous novel, *Lorna Doone*, and it was during a stay on
Exmoor that Coleridge wrote his remarkable poem *Kubla Khan*, in which he mentions ..."that deep romantic chasm
which slanted down a green hill athwart a cedarn cover! A savage place!".

Inset photograph: TARR STEPS, EXMOOR
Standing one metre above the water and spanning some fifty-four metres, this ancient packhorse bridge is an out-
standing example of a clapper bridge. The Tarr Steps consist of seventeen spans formed by flat stone slabs supported
on piers. No-one knows where its massive stone slabs came from, for they certainly aren't local. The bridge was
probably constructed in early medieval times. The name Tarr may derive from *tochar*, meaning causeway.

STONEHENGE, WILTSHIRE
Standing in spectacular isolation on Salisbury Plain, the so-called "Druid" monument of Stonehenge.
Stonehenge was constructed from "sarsens" - local blocks of hard sandstone - and "blue" boulders,
which were transported all the way from the Preseli Mountains in South Wales. Exactly how this was
achieved with the resources available at that time remains an enigma.

Main photograph and inset photograph: UFFINGTON CASTLE AND
WHITE HORSE, OLD BERKSHIRE
Carved in full flight, the Uffington White Horse gallops its way across the crest of its undulating hillside.
Possibly as ancient as the earthwork castle which lies above it, the horse continues to be the subject of local folk-
lore within the communities that live in its shadow.

Main photograph: CHERHILL WHITE HORSE, WILTSHIRE
Cut in 1780 under the direction of Dr Christopher Alsop, the 'mad doctor,' the story goes that, having pegged the rough shape on the hillside with white flags, he then took up a position some two kilometres away and directed the final shape to his men by means of a speaking trumpet.

Inset photographs: ALTON BARNES WHITE HORSE, WILTSHIRE
WESTBURY WHITE HORSE, WILTSHIRE
PEWSEY WHITE HORSE, WILTSHIRE

CROP CIRCLES, WILTSHIRE AND HAMPSHIRE

Inexplicable shapes that appear unseen in the fields of southern England. Elaborate hieroglyphs waiting to be deciphered or elegant confidence trick? Will their secret ever be discovered? This recent phenomenon is assured of a place in Britain's history books.

CERNE GIANT, DORSET
A mysterious sixty metre long figure bearing a giant club stands overlooking the picturesque village of Cerne Abbas. Experts disagree as to the exact date when this impressive figure was carved out of the turf. Many believe that it is a representation of a powerful god dating from Roman Britain, whereas others remain convinced that the figure dates back to a much earlier time and is associated with the fertility rites which were practised at that time.

Main photograph: THE CHAIR, AVEBURY, WILTSHIRE
A fine example of the two categories of stone used at Avebury, the broad stone (female) and the upright (male).

Inset photograph: AVEBURY, WILTSHIRE
The complex at Avebury is Europe's largest Neolithic stone circle. Totalling some two hundred stones, the site consists of two small circles within a larger one. The entire construction is surrounded by massive earthworks and connected to a temple (the Sanctuary) by a long avenue of standing stones. The circle at Avebury dates from 2500-2200 BC, and it is thought that it took centuries to construct. Although the Sanctuary no longer exists, its site is marked by posts.

GLASTONBURY ABBEY, SOMERSET
Although the abbey ruins only date from the 13th century, Joseph of Arimathea is said to have established
Christianity here with the building of England's first church. Legend and folklore, however, lie at the heart of
Glastonbury. Reputed to be Avalon, the burial place of King Arthur and his queen, Guinivere, Glastonbury is
also believed to be the resting place of the Holy Grail.

Main photograph: CASTLE ACRE, NORFOLK
The village of Castle Acre stands within the earthwork defences of an early fortified manor house. The house was replaced in the 11th century by a stone keep, the remains of which are still visible today.

Inset photograph: CASTLE ACRE PRIORY, NORFOLK
A Cluniac monastery was founded here around 1190 by William, second Earl of Warenne, whose father introduced the order into England. The priory ruins provide an impressive example of Norman architecture.

Main and inset photographs: TARN HOWS, CUMBRIA
Surprisingly, although wild in appearance, Tarn Hows was landscaped by the Marshal family, of nearby
Monk Coniston Hall, in the 1850s. The whole estate was put up for sale in 1929 and purchased by Beatrix
Potter in order to save it from development. Tarn Hows, a popular attraction, is now in the care of the
National Trust.

Main photograph: CRUMMOCK WATER, CUMBRIA
"It must be mentioned also, that there is scarcely anything finer than a view from a boat in the centre of Crummock Water. The scene is deep and solemn, and lonely; and in no other spot is the majesty of the Mountains so irresistibly felt..." *William Wordsworth*

Inset photograph: DERWENT WATER, CUMBRIA
Considered by Ruskin to be one of the most beautiful views in Europe. On the lake's west shore is the 108 acre Brandelhow estate, the first property acquired by the National Trust in the Lake District. St. Herbert's Island in Derwent Water bears traces of the home of St. Herbert, a 7th century disciple of St. Cuthbert.

Main photograph: CONISTON WATER, CUMBRIA
The original name of Coniston Water was Turstini Watra (Thorstein's Lake). The lake's present name dates from the time of King Stephen. The area around Coniston has been a focus for industry since antiquity; the Romans had bloomeries, the Furness monks brought mining and forestry, and in the 19th century Coniston became a mining village. The famous peak, the Old Man of Coniston, stands in the background dominating the village and lake.

Inset photograph: WINDERMERE, CUMBRIA
The lake was formed during the ice age by the joining of two glaciers, so that, although the ends are very deep, a shallow, natural bridge lies at Windermere's centre, where the water is only three metres deep in places. At seventeen kilometres long, this is England's largest lake.

CASTLERIGG STONE CIRCLE, CUMBRIA
Set high on a plateau, the thirty-eight boulders of Castlerigg stand encircled by spectacular mountain scenery.
This stone circle is 3,500 years old.

Main photograph: SCA FELL, CUMBRIA
"Cushions or tufts of moss, parched and brown, appear between the huge blocks and stones that lie in heaps on all sides to a great distance, like skeletons or bones of the earth not needed at the creation, and there left to be covered with never dying lichens, which the clouds and dew nourish, and adorn with colours of vivid and exquisite beauty." *Dorothy Wordsworth*

Inset photograph: DOVE COTTAGE, CUMBRIA
Home to Dorothy and William Wordsworth from 1799, Dove Cottage, once an ale house known as the Dove and Olive Bough, still retains much of its original simplicity.

Main photograph and inset: WALLTOWN CRAGS, HADRIAN'S WALL, NORTHUMBERLAND
Stretching about 117 kilometres across England's narrowest point, Hadrian's Wall was the northern frontier of ancient Rome. Over four metres high and one metre wide, the wall is faced with dressed stone and in-filled with puddled earth and clay. Milecastles were erected at every Roman mile (1,480 metres), with two turrets equidistant between each pair of milecastles.

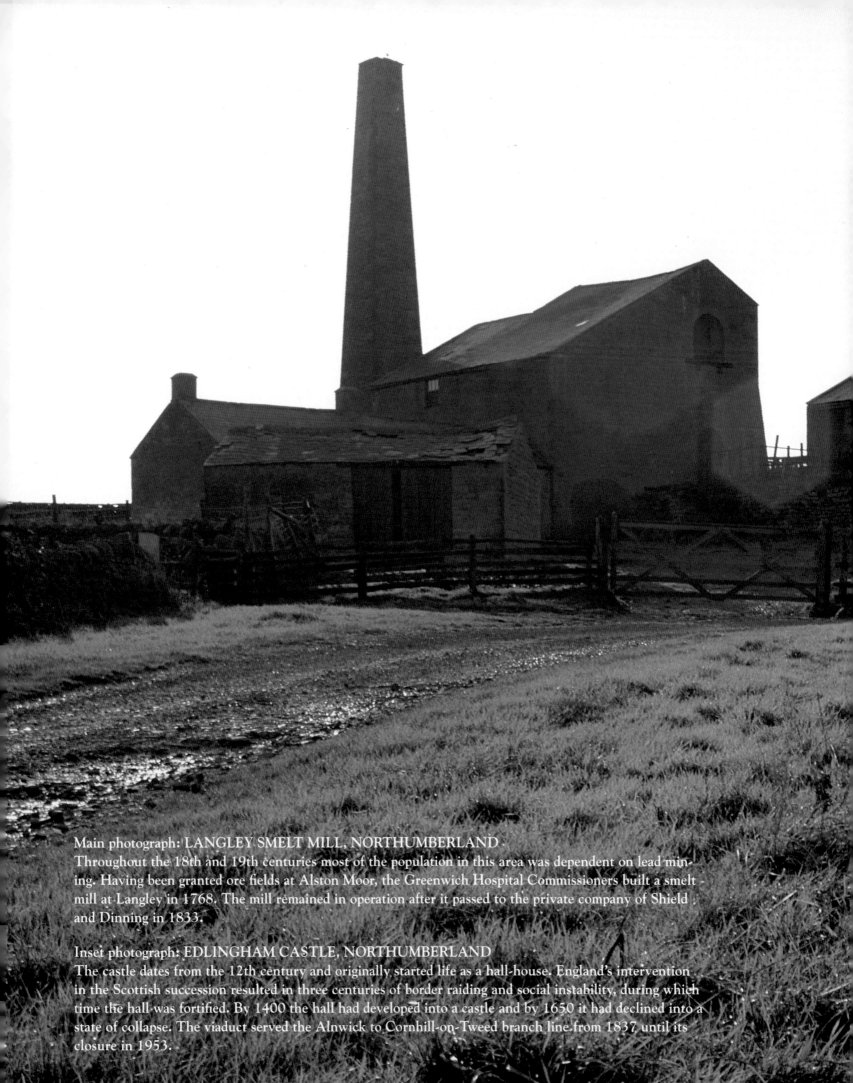

Main photograph: LANGLEY SMELT MILL, NORTHUMBERLAND
Throughout the 18th and 19th centuries most of the population in this area was dependent on lead mining. Having been granted ore fields at Alston Moor, the Greenwich Hospital Commissioners built a smelt mill at Langley in 1768. The mill remained in operation after it passed to the private company of Shield and Dinning in 1833.

Inset photograph: EDLINGHAM CASTLE, NORTHUMBERLAND
The castle dates from the 12th century and originally started life as a hall-house. England's intervention in the Scottish succession resulted in three centuries of border raiding and social instability, during which time the hall was fortified. By 1400 the hall had developed into a castle and by 1650 it had declined into a state of collapse. The viaduct served the Alnwick to Cornhill-on-Tweed branch line from 1837 until its closure in 1953.

MOSSDALE, NORTH YORKSHIRE
Typical of the Pennines landscape, Mossdale is the smallest of the side dales found along the length of Wensleydale. The history of these dales is reflected in the walls and roads which wind their way across this backbone of England, for these routes follow the ancient packhorse trails, established many centuries ago.

WALES

LLANBERIS PASS, GWYNEDD

One of the most beautiful views in Wales. Seen from Llyn Padarn, Snowdonia's largest lake, the Llanberis Pass runs down to the foot of Snowdon. Many Welsh names begin with 'Llan-' which means church. This is frequently followed by the name of the saint to whom the church is dedicated. In the case of Llanberis, the name is that of St. Peris, who is said to have arrived in Wales as a missionary from Rome in the 6th century.

Main photograph: SNOWDON, GWYNEDD
Capped in cloud, Yr Wyddfa (Snowdon) rises 1,085 metres, the highest mountain in Wales and England. Following English invasion in the Middle Ages, Snowdonia served as a formidable stronghold to the Welsh resistance, from which they carried out a series of hit-and-run attacks against the invaders.

Inset photograph: ABERGLASLYN PASS, GWYNEDD
Lying directly south of Snowdon is the spectacular Aberglaslyn Pass. Not so long ago, when the River Glaslyn was tidal, ships could sail directly up the pass between its towering cliffs.

Main and inset photographs: MOUNTAIN STREAMS,
CWM BYCHAN, GWYNEDD

Gwynedd is a county which is rich in history. Protected on
the north and west by the sea, and to the south and east by
mountain ranges, the whole region is a natural fortress,
which, for centuries, resisted penetration by invaders.
When, in 1158, the rulers of the other three kingdoms in
Wales submitted to Henry II, and were reduced to the status
of barons, Owen ap Gwynedd insisted on bearing the title of
prince. In 1267 Llewelyn II, with the permission of
Henry III, declared himself Prince of Wales. It was not until
his death in 1282 that Gwynedd finally fell. Then Edward I
declared his own son Prince of Wales, creating a precedent
which is still followed.

Main photograph: SNOWDONIA, GWYNEDD
The northern peaks of Snowdonia seen across Conwy Bay.

Inset photograph: CAERNARVON BAY, GWYNEDD
Rising straight out of the golden waters of Caernarvon Bay, the peaks of Yr Eifl (The Rivals). The town of
Caernarvon is one of the few places in Britain which has retained its city walls and towers almost intact. Of the
castle built by Edward I on Menai Strait little but the outer shell remains of the thirteen towers and two gate-
ways, but it still offers an impressive sight. The famous Roman fort of Segontium is located to the south east of
Caernarvon.

Main photograph: LLANTHONY VALLEY, BLACK MOUNTAINS, POWYS
Lost in the Vale of Ewyas, Llanthony Valley hides deep in the Black Mountains, watched over
by its 12th century priory.

Inset photograph: LLANTHONY PRIORY, BLACK MOUNTAINS, POWYS
"Here the monks, sitting in their cloisters, enjoying the fresh air, when they happen to look up towards the
horizon, behold the tops of the mountains, as if they were touching the heavens." *Gerald of Wales, 1188*

Main photograph: PRESELI HILLS, DYFED
The whole of the Preseli range is steeped in ancient history. The fact that the altar stone as well as thirty-three blocks at Stonehenge came from here indicates that this region was considered to be sacred in the period from 1600-1400 BC. The countryside around here is dotted with standing stones, stone circles, burial mounds and earthworks.

Inset photograph: PENTRE IFAN, PRESELI HILLS
One of the most impressive tombs in Wales. Built about 4,000 years ago by Neolithic settlers from Ireland, the tomb was originally covered by a mound of earth. Folklore says that, should a maid crawl around a cromlech at full moon, she will see her lover standing in the moonlight. But, should a man fall asleep under the capstone, he will die, go raving mad or become a poet.

Main and inset photograph: PRESELI HILLS, DYFED
Early morning mist on the edge of the Preselis, and a setting full moon at dawn. This is the countryside
across which King Arthur and his companions are said to have hunted Twrch Trwyth, the monstrous boar,
which was once a king, until he was turned into a wild boar as punishment for his evil deeds.

THE BRECON BEACONS, POWYS

Quite unlike the rocky mountains of the north, the green escarpments of the Brecon Beacons undulate gently overlooking lightly wooded valleys. In the churchyard at Llanspyddid in Brecon there is a gravestone which is said to be that of Brychan, the ancient chieftain of the Dark Ages after whom the area of Brecon was named. His daughter, Tydfil, was murdered and subsequently canonised, and the town, Merthyr Tydfil on the southern edge of the Brecon Beacons was named after her.

ST BRYNACH'S CHURCH, NEVERN, DYFED

This corner of old Pembrokeshire simply exudes antiquity. Noteworthy features include the
stones inscribed in both latin and ogham, a mysterious avenue of yew trees and the heavily
decorated 11th century stone cross. The church tower dates from the 12th century and is all that
remains of the early Norman structure.

ST GOVAN'S HEAD AND CHAPEL, DYFED
Perched amongst the rocks, halfway down the cliff face and reached by fifty-two perilously steep stone steps, St Govan's Chapel has been a place of pilgrimage since medieval times. St Govan, a 6th century Irishman from Wexford, is supposed to have landed here and, having built a cell, spent the rest of his days in quiet contemplation.

SCOTLAND

EILEAN NAN RON ISLAND, HIGHLANDS
Lying just off Scotland's northern coastline, below a shifting play of light and cloud, sits the island of
Eilean nan Ron. The coastline in this area is bleak but spectacular, and bears traces of many of
Scotland's earliest inhabitants, particularly those who lived there during the Bronze Age and the era of
Viking rule.

DUNCANSBY HEAD, HIGHLANDS

In the far north of Scotland, just a few kilometres east of John O' Groats, is the spectacular coastline of Duncansby Head. Best viewed along its cliff-top walks, Duncansby offers many examples of nature as sculptress, including Muckle Stack, Peedle Stack and Tom Thumb Stack - collectively, the Stacks of Duncansby (see inset). This area of Scotland was ruled by the Norsemen - the Vikings - until the early 13th century, and many traces of this long period of Norse rule are still evident in Sutherland and Caithness. Indeed, Sutherland was so called because it was "southern land" for the Norsemen, and the "-ness" in Caithness is the Norse word for headland.

Main photograph: THE CUILLIN HILLS, ISLE OF SKYE, HIGHLANDS
The jagged mountain range of The Cuillin Hills contains some of the most dramatic rocks in Scotland, and
certainly in Britain. Although these are scored by ancient ice age glaciers, paradoxically they are also the
youngest rocks in Scotland! The Isle of Skye is probably most famous for providing a safe haven for Bonnie
Prince Charlie. Flora Macdonald rowed him over the channel from the mainland after the Jacobite rebellion
failed when his army was routed by the Duke of Cumberland at Culloden in 1746.

Top Inset photograph: ARDTRECK POINT, ISLE OF SKYE
Looking across Loch Harport towards the beaconed peninsular of Ardtreck Point.

Inset photograph: THE STORR, ISLE OF SKYE
A buttress of rock rears above the Sound of Raasay - The Old Man of Storr. These castle-like towers are the
remains of an eroded terrace of lava.

GLEN BREIN, HIGHLANDS

Glen Brein lies on the southern side of the Great Glen Fault, which runs between Inverness and Fort William, and is typical of many such glens in the region. The town of Fort William grew out of a military depot which was established there in the early 18th century in an attempt to control the rebellious Highlanders who were opposed to the Treaty of Union with England in 1707 and longed for the return of a Stuart king to rule Scotland.

LOCH LOMOND, STRATHCLYDE
The largest stretch of inland water in Britain, Loch Lomond is only one mile from the sea loch, Loch Long, at Arrochar. The Viking leader, Magnus, made his men pull their galleys across that mile and refloat them on Loch Lomond, so that he could burn and pillage the lochside villages. Ben Lomond overlooks the loch on its east side.

LOCH NESS, HIGHLANDS
Each year the loch attracts thousands of visitors who stand and gaze expectantly across the rippled surface
of its impenetrable waters, keen to catch a glimpse of the Loch Ness Monster. The 16th century ruins of
Urquhart Castle, once home to the chiefs of Clan Grant, stand on the lochside.

Main photograph: LOCH GARRY, HIGHLANDS

Glen Garry stretches out into the distance, whilst the waters of Loch Garry wind their way towards the Great Glen. In the town of Invergarry there is a well called the "Well of the Heads" which was named after a famous skirmish between local clans in the 17th century. The heads of seven brothers, who had been killed as reprisal for the murder of one of the chieftain's two sons, were washed in the well and then presented to the chief of their clan. Until the 18th century, the ancient Highland clans were virtually independent kingdoms and their only allegiance was to their chiefs. Central Scottish or English government was a meaningless concept for them. Feuds between clans were frequent and bloody.

Inset photograph: LOCH TARFF, HIGHLANDS

BEN NEVIS, HIGHLANDS
The two central peaks of Aanach Mor and Aanach Beag with Britain's largest mountain, Ben Nevis, to their right, seen across Glen Spean.

LOCH NA H-ACHLAISE, STRATHCLYDE
Loch na h-Achlaise with the snow-capped Clach Leathad reflected in the loch's waters.

Inset photograph: LOCH ACHRAY, CENTRAL
A once secluded loch on the eastern side of the enormously popular Trossachs Pass.

THE TROSSACHS, CENTRAL
Widely considered to include the entire valley containing lochs Katrine, Achray and Vennachar, the true Trossachs Pass is simply the narrow, wooded stretch of land squeezed between lochs Katrine and Achray. Scott's *Lady of the Lake* and *Rob Roy* established the Trossachs as a popular Victorian holiday resort.

Main photograph: LAMMERMUIR HILLS, BORDERS
The rounded outlines of the Lammermuir Hills soften in the evening light. The name Lammermuir means 'lambs' moor', and, although it sounds Scottish, it is actually Old English in origin, from lambra (lamb) and môr (moor). The name of the hills was recorded in a document dating from the year 800 as Lombormore.

Inset photograph: SMAILHOLM TOWER, BORDERS
A 16th century peel tower built to defend against English attacks. An Act of Council from 1587 obliged the owners to "keep watch nyght and day, and burn baillis (bales) according to the accoustomat ordour observit as sic tymes upoun the borderis".

Main photograph: RIVER NITH, DUMFRIES AND GALLOWAY
Rushing between wooded banks, the waters of the River Nith tumble beneath Glenairie Bridge. In ancient
times, although Ayrshire and Dumfriesshire became part of the kingdom of Britons of Strathclyde,
Galloway remained a staunch Pictish province. This independent region sometimes even sided with the
English against the Scots. Galloway was also a great stronghold of the Presbyterians who opposed
Episcopacy in the 17th century.

Inset photograph: LOCH DOON, STRATHCLYDE
The banks of Loch Doon give way to forest as they spread into the surrounding hills. The loch's largest
island, once the site of Doon Castle, was submerged in the 1930s and the castle was rebuilt on the loch's
eastern shore.

HISTORIC PLACES
OF BRITAIN

72
74
74

76
76
76

78

84 82

86

88
88
90
80

GLASGOW EDINBURGH

92
92

94 94

NEWCASTLE
46
48

38 42
38
44 44
40 40
36

50

LEEDS

MANCHESTER

58 52
54
54
56 58

34

BIRMINGHAM

64
62 68

60
60

66

SWANSEA

22
22
30
24 24
26 24
24
20

LONDON

CARDIFF BRISTOL
32
24

18
18

26

28

16

10 10
14
12 12

8

© The Automobile Association 1994